Diana Ross

The Voice That Touched the World

J.D MAX

Table of Contents

Prologue

The Queen of Motown - Diana Ross

For many people, this name means more than just a singer. It means beauty, success, and courage. Diana Ross is a woman who changed music history forever. She showed the world that dreams could come true even for a young girl from Detroit.

For more than sixty years, Diana Ross's voice has touched millions of hearts. As the lead singer of The Supremes, she helped create the famous "Motown Sound" that changed pop and soul music. Her songs played on radios everywhere, from small towns to big cities, making people dance, sing, and smile. She became a star shining brighter than almost anyone in her time.

But Diana Ross's life was not always easy. She faced many struggles on her way to success.

Fame brought joy, but also sadness and hard choices. She worked hard every day to reach the top. She broke many barriers that stood in the way of young Black artists. She proved that talent, style, and hard work could open any door.

This book is not only about music or fame. It is about the woman behind the songs, the daughter, the friend, the dreamer. It is about her strength, her mistakes, her victories, and her lasting mark on the world.

This is the story of Diana Ross the Queen of Motown. A story that still inspires people today.

Chapter One

Growing Up in Detroit

The Early Years

Diana Ross was born on March 26, 1944, in Detroit, Michigan. Her full name at birth was Diana Ernestine Earle Ross. She was the second of six children in a working-class family. Her father, Fred Ross, Sr., worked as a laborer, and her mother, Ernestine, was a schoolteacher. Life in Detroit was not rich or easy, but the Ross family was close and full of love.

Diana grew up in a neighborhood called Brewster-Douglass housing projects. These were tall, crowded buildings where many African-American families lived. The area was poor, but it was also full of life, music, and community spirit. In the evenings, neighbors gathered on porches or street corners, sharing stories and singing. Gospel music filled the air from local churches. The sound of soul, jazz, and blues came from record players and radios.

Even as a small girl, Diana loved to sing. She sang at home, at school, and at church. Her family noticed her beautiful voice. She was shy at times but came alive when she sang. Music made her happy. It made her dream of a bigger, brighter world outside the walls of her Detroit home.

In school, Diana was a good student. She liked fashion, sewing, and design. She dreamed of becoming a fashion designer. But music kept calling her. She listened to singers like Mahalia Jackson and Billie Holiday and imagined herself on stage someday. When she sang along with records, her voice was clear, strong, and sweet.

As a teenager, Diana attended Cass Technical High School, a school known for its music and arts programs. There she met other students who also loved music, including Florence Ballard and Mary Wilson. Together, they started singing after school. Their voices blended perfectly, creating beautiful harmonies. They called themselves "The Primettes", the sister group to a male Motown group called "The Primes" (which later became The Temptations).

Diana and her friends dreamed of making records and becoming famous. They performed at local talent shows and parties. People began to notice them. Their clothes were homemade, their microphones borrowed, but their sound was full of promise.

At first, no one thought a group of young Black girls from the Detroit projects could become stars. The music industry was hard, especially for women of color. But Diana and her friends were determined. They believed in their talent. They practiced every day, trying to perfect their moves, their voices, their songs.

In 1960, the girls got their first chance to audition for Berry Gordy, the founder of Motown Records. He was building a new kind of music empire in Detroit, one that could bring Black artists into the homes of all Americans. Berry Gordy saw something special in Diana Ross. He signed the group to Motown but only after asking them to wait until they finished high school.

This small moment would change Diana's life forever.

Soon, The Primettes became The Supremes, and their journey to stardom would begin.

But before the fame, before the number one hits, before the bright lights, Diana Ross was just a girl from Detroit, a girl with a big dream and a bigger voice.

Her story was only beginning.

Chapter Two

The Birth of The Supremes

From School Friends to Motown Stars

In the early 1960s, the music world was changing fast. A new sound was rising from the heart of Detroit, a sound called Motown. And in the middle of this exciting time were four teenage girls with big dreams: Diana Ross, Florence Ballard, Mary Wilson, and Betty McGlown. Together, they formed a group called The Primettes.

Diana and her friends were full of hope. They sang at local events, talent shows, and school parties. They wore homemade dresses and shared one old microphone between them. They didn't have fancy equipment or managers. But they had something better: beautiful harmony and a desire to succeed.

The Primettes wanted to become part of the new Motown family. In 1960, they gathered the courage to audition for Berry Gordy, the head of Motown Records. At that time, Berry Gordy had already signed young stars like Smokey Robinson and Marvin Gaye. The girls hoped he would see their talent too.

Berry Gordy liked their sound, but he thought they were too young and inexperienced. He asked them to finish high school first. It was a big disappointment. But the girls didn't give up. They kept performing, practicing, and improving their style. They were patient.

After some time, Betty McGlown left the group, and a new member, Barbara Martin, joined. Soon after, Berry Gordy finally gave them a contract with Motown but with a new name. The Primettes were now called The Supremes. The name sounded elegant, classy, and full of promise. It was a name that would soon become famous all over the world.

In the beginning, success was not easy. Their first records were not hits. The Supremes became known as the "no-hit Supremes" at Motown because none of their early songs made the charts. It was frustrating. Other Motown artists like The Temptations and The Miracles were having big hits, but The Supremes were still waiting for their chance.

But Diana, Florence, and Mary did not give up. They worked hard in the studio, recording song after song. They trained in the famous Motown "Artist Development" school, where they learned how to walk, talk, dress, and perform like true stars. Motown wanted its artists to be the best not just in sound, but in style and class.

In 1962, Barbara Martin left the group. From that point on, The Supremes became a trioDiana Ross, Florence Ballard, and Mary Wilson. The three girls became close, like sisters. They shared dreams, laughter, and fears. They also faced competition, jealousy, and pressure. Being a young woman in the music business was not easy.

Then in 1964, everything changed.

Motown's top songwriting team, Holland-Dozier-Holland, gave The Supremes a song called "Where Did Our Love Go." At first, the girls didn't like the song. They thought it was too simple, too childish. But they recorded it anyway. When the song was released, it surprised everyone it went straight to number one on the Billboard Hot 100 chart.

The Supremes had finally found their magic sound.

After that, the hits kept coming: "Baby Love," "Come See About Me," "Stop! In the Name of Love," "Back in My Arms Again." Each song became a hit. The Supremes broke record after record. They became the first American group to have five number-one singles in a row. No one man or woman had done that before.

America fell in love with The Supremes. Young girls wanted to dress like them, sing like them, and be like them. The group appeared on TV shows like The Ed Sullivan Show, performing for millions of viewers. Their elegant gowns, perfect hair, and graceful moves set new standards for beauty and style.

Diana Ross was becoming the star of the group. Her soft, clear voice and charming smile made her stand out. Berry Gordy saw this. He began to push Diana to the front as the lead singer, while Florence and Mary sang backup. This decision made The Supremes even more successful but it also created tension among the three friends. Florence and Mary sometimes felt left behind as Diana's fame grew.

Even with these troubles, The Supremes were on top of the world. They toured the United States, played sold-out concerts, and even performed in Europe and Asia. They opened doors for other Black artists and broke racial barriers in the music industry. Before The Supremes, few Black women had reached such fame in mainstream pop music.

The Supremes became not just singers but symbols of hope. At a time when the United States was struggling with racial injustice, The Supremes showed that talent and hard work could overcome prejudice. They proved that young Black women could lead the charts and win the hearts of all AmericansBlack and white.

But behind the glitter and success, problems were growing. The tension between Diana, Florence, and Mary was becoming worse. Berry Gordy was giving more attention to Diana, preparing her for a solo career. Florence Ballard felt pushed aside. Mary Wilson felt caught in the middle. The close friendship they once shared was slowly falling apart.

Still, at this moment in the mid-1960s, The Supremes were at their peak. They were the queens of Motown. Their songs played everywhere. Their smiles lit up the stage. And Diana Ross's little Diana from Detroit was on her way to becoming a superstar.

Their story was far from over.

Chapter Three

Breaking Records and Barriers

The Supremes Conquer the World

By 1965, The Supremes were no longer just a group from Detroit, they were world-famous stars. Their songs topped music charts in the United States, the United Kingdom, and many other countries. Fans everywhere knew their names. Young girls copied their hairstyles and fashion. Magazines wrote stories about them. TV shows invited them to perform. The Supremes had become a part of pop culture.

At this time, the music world was mostly led by white artists like The Beatles, Elvis Presley, and The Beach Boys. But The Supremes broke this pattern. They became the first Black female group to reach the top of the charts again and again. Their success was a big step forward for African-American musicians in a world where racial barriers still stood strong.

Their music was full of joy, heartbreak, and charm. Songs like "You Can't Hurry Love", "You Keep Me Hangin' On", and "Love Is Here and Now You're Gone" became big hits. Each song told a simple but touching story about love, waiting, or disappointment that everyone could understand. People of all ages, races, and countries sang along with their music.

As the group's fame grew, they began to tour not only across America but around the world. The Supremes performed in Europe, Asia, and even Australia. Crowds cheered for them wherever they went. Fans waited for hours just to catch a glimpse of Diana Ross, Florence Ballard, and Mary Wilson. They became symbols of style and class, always dressed in beautiful, sparkling gowns, their hair perfect, their smiles bright.

They also performed in some places where Black artists were rarely allowed to perform before. In the United States, many theaters and hotels had once refused to let Black entertainers stay or sing. But The Supremes broke these rules. When they performed at the famous Copacabana nightclub in New York City, they made history. Before them, very few Black performers had been invited to that stage. The Supremes' appearance there opened doors for many other African-American artists in the years to come.

Behind the scenes, however, things were not as perfect as they looked. The success of The Supremes brought new problems.

One big change was happening quietlyDiana Ross was becoming the clear leader of the group. Berry Gordy, the head of Motown Records, wanted Diana to be the star. He thought her voice and charm would take the group even further. As a result, Florence and Mary were pushed into the background. This caused sadness and anger, especially for Florence Ballard, who had helped start the group. She felt forgotten.

The tension grew worse as Berry Gordy made plans for Diana's solo career. The Supremes were slowly changing into "Diana Ross & The Supremes." Even the group's name was changed to show that Diana was the main focus. This broke the hearts of the other members. They had worked so hard together, but now it seemed like they were only there to support Diana's rise to the top.

In 1967, the tension reached its peak. Florence Ballard was struggling. She missed shows, drank too much, and argued with the others. Finally, she was asked to leave the group. A new singer, Cindy Birdsong, replaced her. It was the end of the original Supremes.

Fans were shocked. The perfect image of The Supremes was breaking apart behind the glittering stage lights.

But the music kept coming. With Diana as the clear leader, The Supremes scored more hits, like "Reflections" and "Someday We'll Be Together." Their songs became more serious, reflecting the changing times. America was going through big social changes, the civil rights movement, the Vietnam War, protests, and unrest. Even pop music began to carry deeper messages.

Despite these changes, The Supremes' music remained popular. People needed beauty and joy in difficult times, and The Supremes gave them both.

By now, Diana Ross was more than just the voice of The Supremes. She was a star all by herself. She appeared on magazine covers. She met famous people like President Lyndon Johnson, movie stars, and other great musicians. Berry Gordy believed that Diana could become not only a music star but a movie star too.

The end of the 1960s brought a big moment: Diana Ross was about to leave The Supremes and start her solo career. The group that had conquered the world together was about to split. The friendship that had started in Detroit schoolyards was over.

But their place in music history was already safe. The Supremes had changed everything.

They proved that young Black women could rule the music world. They inspired thousands of other artists. They broke walls and opened doors. They showed grace, power, and endless style.

And at the center of it all was Diana Rossa quiet girl from Detroit who was now ready to shine on her own.

Chapter Four

Going Solo

Diana Ross Finds Her Own Path

By 1970, it was officialDiana Ross was leaving
The Supremes. After years of singing with the
group, after breaking records and making
history, Diana was ready to walk a new road as a
solo artist. It was a brave step. No one knew for
sure if she could succeed on her own. The music
world was changing fast, and new stars were
rising. But Diana believed in herself. So did
Berry Gordy, the head of Motown Records.

Motown planned her solo career carefully. They
wanted Diana to shine, to be more than just a
former Supreme. Berry Gordy gave her the best
producers, the best songwriters, and the best
promotion. Motown spent a lot of money to
make sure the world noticed Diana Ross the solo
singer.

Her first solo single was "Reach Out and Touch (Somebody's Hand)". It was not a number one hit, but it was a gentle, hopeful song that many fans loved. Soon after, Diana released "Ain't No Mountain High Enough"a song that changed everything. With its spoken parts and powerful singing, the song went to number one on the Billboard Hot 100 chart. Diana Ross had proven that she could make it without The Supremes.

More hits followed. Songs like "Touch Me in the Morning," "Love Hangover," and "It's My House" showed Diana's soft and emotional side. Her music covered pop, soul, and disco styles. She could sing a gentle ballad or an exciting dance song. No matter the style, Diana's voice was always full of feeling and beauty.

But Diana wanted more than just music success. She dreamed of becoming a movie star. Berry Gordy also wanted this for her. In 1972, Diana starred in her first major film, "Lady Sings the Blues," a movie about the tragic life of jazz singer Billie Holiday. Many people doubted that

Diana could act. But she surprised everyone with her strong, emotional performance. The movie was a hit, and Diana was nominated for an Academy Award (Oscar) for Best Actress. Few singers had ever crossed into acting so successfully.

After that, Diana starred in more films, including "Mahogany" in 1975, where she played a poor woman who becomes a famous fashion designer. The movie's theme song, "Do You Know Where You're Going To", became another hit single. In 1978, she starred in "The Wiz", a modern version of The Wizard of Oz with an all-Black cast. Diana played Dorothy, and the film became a favorite, especially in the African-American community.

In the late 1970s and early 1980s, Diana Ross also became the Queen of Disco. Her song "Upside Down" in 1980, produced by the famous band Chic, was a worldwide hit. Everyone danced to it in clubs and on the radio. Her next big song, "I'm Coming Out", became an anthem, especially for the LGBTQ+ community, because its words spoke of freedom and self-expression.

Diana's career seemed unstoppable. She moved from Motown Records to RCA Records in 1981, signing a record-breaking contract worth millions of dollars. She released more albums, went on world tours, and stayed in the public eye. Her concerts were grand and exciting. Fans came from everywhere to see her live.

But life as a solo superstar was not always easy. Diana had to work hard to stay at the top. She was now alone on stage, without her old friends Florence and Mary. The pressure was heavy. Every album, every film, every concert had to succeed. People expected perfection from her.

Her personal life also had its ups and downs. Diana married twice and raised five children. Being a mother and a superstar was not simple. She spent long months away from home on tours. The newspapers wrote about her relationships, her marriages, and her family problems. But through all this, Diana kept smiling in public. She protected her private life as best she could.

Even with these struggles, Diana never stopped working. She recorded duet songs with famous artists like Lionel Richie, including the worldwide hit "Endless Love" in 1981. The song became one of the biggest love songs of all time, played at weddings and romantic events everywhere.

Diana also gave back to the community. She supported charities, especially those for children, education, and AIDS awareness. She became a role model not only for singers but for young women, showing that strength, style, and independence were possible for Black women in a world that did not always welcome them.

By the end of the 1980s, Diana Ross had become more than just a pop star. She was an iconic symbol of grace, success, and survival. Her music, her films, and her fashion made her one of the most famous women in the world.

And even as music changed with time, Diana stayed true to herself. She adapted to new sounds, new styles, and new audiences. She showed the world that a true artist could last for decades, not just years.

Her solo path was full of risk and hard work. But Diana Ross walked that path with courage. She built a career that stood strong, with or without The Supremes.

Her light kept shining.

And the world kept watching.

Chapter Five

Challenges Behind the Spotlight

Struggles, Strength, and Survival

To the world, Diana Ross seemed perfect. She had the looks, the voice, the fame, and the fortune. Her songs were everywhere. Her movies played in theaters. Her face was on magazine covers. But behind the lights and glamour, Diana faced struggles that the public did not always see.

Being a superstar is not easy. It means long hours, endless travel, sleepless nights, and heavy pressure to stay successful. For Diana Ross, these pressures started early during her years with The Supremes and they grew even bigger when she became a solo artist.

One of Diana's greatest personal struggles was her loneliness. Fame can make life exciting, but it can also make life lonely. Friends become harder to trust. People want something from you: money, favors, fame. True friends become rare. Diana often kept her feelings private. She smiled for the cameras but held her sadness inside.

Her family was important to her. Diana married Robert Ellis Silberstein in 1971. They had two daughters together, Tracee Ellis Ross (who later became a famous actress) and Chudney Ross. Diana also had a daughter, Rhonda Ross Kendrick, whose father was Berry Gordy. Being a mother made Diana happy, but it was also hard. Her busy career kept her far from home. She missed birthdays, school events, and quiet family times. The guilt of being away from her children was a heavy weight on her heart.

In the 1980s, Diana married Arne Naess Jr., a wealthy businessman from Norway. They had two sons together. But this marriage also ended in divorce. Love was not simple in Diana's life.

Fame made relationships harder. Privacy was almost impossible. The media followed her everywhere, writing stories, some true, some not about her love life.

There were also career struggles. Not every album was a hit. Not every film was a success. Critics sometimes wrote harsh reviews. New artists like Whitney Houston and Madonna arrived, capturing the spotlight. The music world was changing fast. Staying on top became harder for Diana.

But Diana Ross did not give up. When things got difficult, she worked harder. She released new albums. She toured the world. She tried new styles, from disco to soul to pop ballads. She showed the world that a true star does not fade easily.

There were public mistakes, too. In 1999, Diana was arrested at an airport for behaving badly with security staff. The story made news headlines. Some fans were shocked. But Diana apologized and moved forward. Like every person, she was not perfect. She made mistakes, but she took responsibility for them.

Perhaps Diana's greatest personal battle was with the feeling of being misunderstood. She wanted to be seen not only as a glamorous singer or movie star but as a strong woman, a caring mother, and a serious artist. Sometimes the public only saw the surface, the gowns, the makeup, the hair. But Diana wanted to be remembered for her music, her passion, and her courage.

Diana also faced the pain of losing old friends. In later years, she made peace with Mary Wilson, her former Supremes partner. But when Florence Ballard died young, in 1976, Diana was deeply saddened. Florence had been her friend in the old Detroit days, before the fame, before the world knew their names. The loss reminded Diana of how far they had all come and what had been lost along the way.

In private moments, Diana spoke of these feelings. In interviews and books, she shared some of her thoughts. She admitted that fame could be a lonely place. But she also said that music saved her life many times. Singing brought her joy. The love of her fans gave her strength.

Through every struggle, Diana Ross kept her head high. She refused to let troubles defeat her. She stayed graceful. She stayed kind. She stayed strong.

Even when the world around her changed, even when her songs no longer topped the charts, Diana's spirit did not break.

She became not just a survivor but a symbol of survival.

A woman who lived through joy and pain, hope and loss and kept shining.

Her life showed that success is not only about awards or money. It is about courage, patience, and believing in yourself when others doubt you.

And that is why Diana Ross's story remains special not just because she sang beautiful songs but because she lived a beautiful, brave life.

Chapter Six

A Living Legend

Diana Ross's Lasting Legacy

Diana Ross is more than a famous singer or a glamorous star. She is a legendary woman whose life and work changed the world of music forever. Her voice, her style, her strength, and her courage made her a symbol of success for people everywhere, especially for young Black women who once thought their dreams were too big.

Even after decades in the spotlight, Diana Ross's influence can still be seen and felt in the music industry. Young artists like Beyoncé, Mariah Carey, Janet Jackson, and Alicia Keys have all said that Diana inspired them. Her songs, her confidence on stage, and her grace opened the door for these women to reach their own dreams. Without Diana, the path for these superstars might have been harder or longer.

Diana also changed the way the world saw beauty and fashion. Her shining gowns, perfect hair, and elegant moves set a new standard for glamour. She showed that a Black woman could lead the fashion world just as much as the music world. Magazines featured her face. Fashion designers made clothes for her. Fans around the world copied her style.

But Diana's true legacy is not only in music or fashion, it is in the hearts of people who found hope in her story.

She came from a poor neighborhood in Detroit, the daughter of simple, hardworking parents. She faced hard times, rejection, doubt, and struggle. Yet she did not stop. She kept dreaming. She kept working. She turned her dreams into reality. For millions of fans, this was her greatest giftthe example of never giving up.

Over the years, Diana received many awards and honors. She was given a Grammy Lifetime Achievement Award, a Kennedy Center Honor, and the title of "Female Entertainer of the Century" by Billboard Magazine. In 2012, she was awarded the Presidential Medal of Freedom, the highest honor for an American civilian. These awards recognized not only her music but her impact on culture and history.

Even today, Diana Ross still performs. She sings in concerts, records albums, and appears at special events. Her voice remains strong. Her smile still lights up the stage. Fans, both young and old, come to see her, sing along to her hits, and remember the golden age of Motown.

But Diana's story is not just about the past. It also teaches lessons for the future. She showed that women, especially Black women, could lead, inspire, and break barriers in a world that often tried to hold them back. She proved that success comes from courage, hard work, and belief in oneself not just luck or beauty.

Her songs like "Ain't No Mountain High Enough" and "I'm Coming Out" still play at parties, weddings, and on the radio. They remind people that dreams are possible. They remind people to rise, to shine, to keep going no matter what life brings.

Diana Ross also became a loving mother and grandmother. Her family grew over the years. Her daughter Tracee Ellis Ross became a famous actress, starring in TV shows like "Black-ish." Through her children, Diana's influence continued into a new generation.

Many wonder what makes Diana Ross so special. Is it her voice? Her beauty? Her charm? The answer is simple: it is her heart. Her strength. Her endless spirit.

She made history not because everything was easy but because she refused to give up when things were hard.

In the end, Diana Ross's life is not only a story of fame and fortune. It is a story of human courage. It is the story of a dream that came true and kept shining for more than sixty years.

Diana Ross is not just a star of the past. She is a living legend. A queen whose crown was earned with talent, struggle, and grace.

And her light still shines.

Epilogue

The Endless Influence of Diana Ross

The story of Diana Ross is more than a story of music. It is the story of a life that touched the world, a life that gave hope, beauty, and strength to millions.

Even now, after more than sixty years in the spotlight, Diana Ross remains a name that means something special. Her voice still plays on the radio. Her songs are still sung at weddings, parties, and celebrations. Young singers still dream of becoming like her. Fashion designers still talk about her style. Fans across the world still smile when they hear her name.

Diana Ross showed the world that dreams can come true, no matter where you start. She was a little girl from Detroit's Brewster-Douglass housing projects, full of hope, full of dreams. She wanted to sing, to be seen, to make her mark. Many people said it was impossible. But Diana proved them wrong. With hard work, courage, and faith, she built a life that few could ever imagine.

Her journey was not always easy. She faced rejection. She lost friends. She felt lonely. But she stood strong. She kept singing, kept smiling, kept believing. Her story reminds us that greatness comes not from a perfect life but from the strength to rise after every fall.

The music world is full of stars who rise and fall, who shine for a short time and then disappear. But Diana Ross is different. Her light has not faded. She is more than a starshe is a legend. Her voice, her songs, her gracethey are part of history now. They will live on for years to come.

For the young girl sitting in her bedroom, dreaming of being on stage...

For the singer practicing in secret, afraid to be heard...
For the woman facing doubts and fears...
Diana Ross is a reminder: You can do it. You can rise. You can shine.

Her story teaches us to believe in ourselves. To keep going. To never give up.

Diana Ross gave the world not only music but also hope.

And that is a gift that will never end.

Printed in Dunstable, United Kingdom